108 Ways
TO EMBODY YOUR MAGNIFICENCE

Many of us go about our days *in* a daze. When we are not fully aware of how we're thinking, we get distracted and pulled off center. It serves us well to become more aware of our thoughts, and to infuse them with loving consciousness. This consciousness brings us back to the core.

Some of the ideas presented in this book may feel like new ways of thinking. In truth, they represent our most empowered perspective. They center on the truth of who you are. I offer these *108 Ways* as loving reminders that your magnificence transcends personality, because *your divine essence is magnificence.*

It is my great pleasure to share this with you. May it inspire you to awaken to the fullness of your being.

With Great Love,

Dr. Sue

DR. SUE MORTER
CREATOR OF THE ENERGY CODES®

1. Recognize that you are an eternal energy being.

You are made of energy and energy cannot be created or destroyed. You are here having an energetic or spiritual experience.

You may have heard the statement, "You are not a physical being having a spiritual experience, rather you are a spiritual being having a physical experience." Let's take it one step further:

You are a Spiritual being having a Spiritual experience in the physical dimension.

"You are made of energy and energy cannot be created or destroyed."

2. Recognize that Everything is energy — not just you and your nature, but everything in your life.

Energy vibrates in various frequencies. Your thoughts, feelings, and emotions are all energies in various states of vibration, like different radio stations. You can modify these frequencies and shift your emotional states by learning how to move energy through your physical system with freedom and ease.

Take a deep breath from low inside your body (in the belly, lower than you normally breathe) and open to this truth:

I can change the frequency of the energy that moves through this body and through my life with my freewill.

As you breathe into this, it begins to happen automatically. Practice this daily.

3. Deep inside, you know.

Eleven billion bits of information bombard your energy field every millisecond. Most of these pieces of information report to your gut, not to your head.

Trust your gut feeling, because it is based on significantly more information than the clearest thought you can think.

"Trust your gut feeling, because it is based on significantly more information than the clearest thought you can think."

4. KNOW THAT WE ARE IN THIS TOGETHER.

Come from the space of oneness and unity: *I belong, and so do you.*

When we separate ourselves, we perceive the need to protect ourselves. From a perception of separateness, we live in a state of guardedness, constantly listening and looking for the next threat.

Just for this moment, allow yourself to take in this possibility:

We are all on the same side, assisting, learning, nudging, and awakening.

"We are all on the same side, assisting, learning, nudging, and awakening."

5. Shift your thoughts and words — to Creatorship.

Notice when you find yourself speaking from a victim standpoint.

Observe when you think and say things like, "This is just the way it is... There's nothing I can do about it... I don't know what to do... I don't know how to change things... It simply isn't working very well for me... This is just the way I am..."

Over time, those types of victimizing statements can reprogram your subconscious into believing that you are less than whole.

Perceive yourself as full of possibility. Allow yourself to imagine one impossible thing, possible every day. Today, choose one thing to see today from a Yes perspective:

Of course, I can... I'm sure I do... Let's take one step into it and see...

6. Meditate (yes, you can).

Many people think they can't meditate, that they're not very good at it. The mind wanders. Sound familiar? Meditation is a skill, and anyone can learn how and benefit from it.

In meditation, we simply reside in the present moment, observe thoughts as they arise, release them, and return to our point of focus on the present moment.

If you are visual, put a candle in front of you and simply watch the flame, observing its every nuance and movement, without any thought. Just observe.

If you're more kinesthetic, meaning you engage well by doing things physically, choose an internal action such as breathing to be the center of your focus. Simply pay attention to your breath. Follow it in and out the nose, breathe slowly.

As you meditate, imagine the breath moving slowly up and down through the central core channel of the body, in front of the spine, from head to toe and back again. Hearing and following the breath as it moves through the center of the body gives the mind something to do, something to focus on in this present moment.

If you are auditory, repeat a mantra or a phrase. This, too, gives the mind something to do. Repeat something that feels sacred to you: *I Am...* or *God...* or *Love...*

For ten minutes a day, simply allow yourself to be present. With this gift, a beautiful relationship between your inner wisdom and your discerning mind begins to develop, which will enhance the ease with which you can be lovingly present in all the other relationships in your life.

Meditate; don't contemplate. Just sit and *be* for ten minutes a day.

7. BREATHE CONSCIOUSLY.

Focus on drawing the breath long, low, and deep into the body.

We tend to live in our heads. Learn how to draw the energy down into the body instead of collecting it up in the head.

With a deep breath in, the belly comes out like a big Buddha belly over your belt, at the top of your pants. Just allow it to roll out, big and relaxed. On an exhale, draw the belly back toward the spine. As you do this, empty, empty, empty everything out.

When we breathe into the upper lobes of the lungs – as many of us do habitually and unconsciously – we activate an emergency "fight or flight" response. When we draw our breath down into the belly, we breathe into the lower lobes of the lungs, and this cultivates sensations of creativity, relaxation, and well-being.

8. CONSCIOUSLY EXPERIENCE THE SENSATION OF LOVE IN THE BODY.

Create the sensation of love in the body. Ask yourself...

What does it feel like when I am loving?

What do my cells feel like?

What is the vibration that runs through my system when I just practice loving?

Simply generate the sensation of love twenty times a day, even forty times a day – every moment you don't have to be doing something else!

Build a cellular familiarity with this vibration, and soon it becomes a default frequency, the automatic baseline from which you function.

9. Practice Mula Bandha

The ancient Sanskrit term *Mula Bandha* means
"root lock." Practicing a "locking in" of the
energy source all the way down to the tip of the
spine – your root – can help you draw upon a
great deal more energy throughout the day.

When you feel more energized, patience and
stamina also increase, and your emotional
states gravitate more readily toward sensations
of well-being.

Next time you find yourself thinking of
something that troubles you, simply and lovingly
engage *Mula Bandha*. Contract the muscles deep
in the pelvic bowl and squeeze all of the muscles
at the base of the spine. Slightly constrict the
tissues at the perineum, all around the bladder.
Squeeze at the core of your body and begin to
breathe up and down the central core of your
body. Breathe from above your head, through
the throat, the center of the chest, into the belly,
all the way down through the tip of the spine.

Imagine the breath coming up and down the body as you breathe, and negative thoughts will more readily dissipate. You can do this almost any time – while you're driving a car, sitting at the computer, or walking. Just begin to practice drawing this energy down into body.

Energy anchored throughout the whole body helps calm a "runaway mind." The moment you begin to engage this squeezing at the base of the spine, you bring your consciousness more fully into the body. Your loving consciousness in the body helps dissolve and transmute any upset.

"Energy anchored throughout the whole body helps calm a 'runaway mind.'"

10. REMEMBER YOUR SOULFUL CONTRACTS (EVEN IF YOU DON'T "REMEMBER" THEM)

Before entering the theatre of this life experience, you made some requests from behind-the-scenes. You agreed upon these "Soulful Contracts" to assist your awakening to the magnificence that you truly are.

Remember your Soulful Contracts. You may not recall making them, though you can easily recognize them playing out. When you experience agitation or irritation (and joy and exhilaration, too) in a relationship; in a dynamic; in a work situation; choose to see it from a new point of view. "The friction I feel is part of a refinement, a polishing happening for me... *just as I requested.*"

You begin to awaken to this version of you as you penetrate the illusory idea that you are "less than" or lacking in some way, that you could be insufficient or inadequate. These illusions are like veils you must pierce to wake up to your life purpose.

Recognizing that you chose to come here and awaken is part of your life purpose. The Life Purpose is to awaken to your magnificence as a creator, co-creating this life experience, breath by breath, day by day.

"You agreed upon these "Soulful Contracts" to assist your awakening to the magnificence that you truly are."

11. Think in terms of "We"

Think and talk in terms of "We" as often as you can.

Some of us orient our thoughts mostly to the individual self, to "me."

Some of us think of others most of the time, wanting and constantly attempting to please and serve other people.

Both inclinations benefit from more "We" thinking (and speaking). For the "selfish," bringing in more "We" expands our orientation. For the "self-less," more "We" ensures more "me" at the same time.

We receive great benefit when we think in terms of "We," because as quantum science shows us, "We" are One.

"Think and talk in terms of "We" as often as you can."

12. KNOW THAT ULTIMATE FULFILLMENT COMES FROM WITHIN.

Engagement in addictive patterns does not really serve a state of wholeness, wellness, and balance in our lives. If you or someone you know suffers from such imbalances, know that it is not a "bad" thing. It is simply that the light of awareness has not yet shined on some part of this whole person. When we feel imbalanced, we can repetitively seek satiation through external behaviors and substances.

When you feel caught in addictive thinking or behavior, recognize it results from a denial of loving presence for some part of yourself. Know, too, that you are the generator of that loving presence and you are the recipient.

Ultimate fulfillment comes from within. Take your attention inside the body. Bring your concentration deeper into the core of your being than you have let it land before. Then bring your loving attention into your core with deep sincerity, and breathe compassion.

13. LOVE INTO ALL YOUR EMOTIONS — THE HEAVY ONES, TOO.

Recognize that emotions such as guilt and shame, fear and anxiety, all serve a purpose. When we judge and resist emotional states and dispositions, we deny some of our authenticity.

There is nothing more healing than being your authentic self. Celebrate you being you, including the full range of your emotional experience. The mind doesn't want to accept emotions like guilt and shame because we have been taught that they are bad or wrong. We fear that if we accept them, they'll stick around forever. The truth is that only by fully accepting them will they ever dissolve into love.

When feeling any kind of disposition that you do not like or that you wish you did not feel, see if you can manage to love into it and be compassionate with yourself to a deeper degree than you have ever been before. Do not try to get rid of it, simply embrace it. Regard it with

the tenderness and compassion with which you would a hurt child or pet. Allow it, accept it, and breathe.

Still feeling something you wish you didn't? Quantum Science shows us that emotional states like guilt, shame, fear, and anxiety may represent vibrational frequencies that still serve you. Low vibrational states of heavy emotions can actually ground us temporarily until we learn to ground ourselves consciously.

Lovingly embrace all that you are and all that you feel.

"Celebrate you being you, including the full range of your emotional experience."

14. IDENTIFY AS A SPIRIT NOW.

Instead of being a personality that has a Soul, be a Soul that has a personality.

Instead of being a person that has a Spirit, be a Spirit with an engaging outer self exchanging with the world.

Allow what's going to leave this world and go on to the next to be You! Identify with the Spirit now, so that you are identifying as the eternal being that you truly are. When we do so, we more easily retrain, modify, and shift without personal attachment. Then our less-than-loving, not-so-collaborative personality traits begin to shift into alignment with the true masterful Self.

Why wait for some glorious afterlife experience? Allow it to be here now.

15. STEP INTO YOUR POWER.

We thought that power was associated with assertive strength and going out to make things happen. A greater power lives within you. Allow it to shine through the old circuits that were put in place for survival.

Your true power recognizes you are made of creative source energy, that you are a being of light and high frequency energy in the body. As that high frequency energy comes into form, it generates a gentle vibration that we call Love. Find your power in that part of you.

Find power in being gentle and strength in being kind.

Slow yourself into a true version of you.

Step into your power by listening, by being present, by being still.

16. Stop judging your emotional states altogether.

The soulful self finds interest and worth in the entire range of human experience. It is here to learn to embrace it all, not to cut out half of personhood in an attempt to be whole.

Have what you have. If you find yourself upset, allow the upset. Your consent brings love, and your conscious attention assures responsible stewardship so the upset need not be projected onto another. Feel the energy of the upset, and breathe it through the body – through and through, literally up and down the central core of your being, from head to toe and up again.

Breathing in this way, we build a loving relationship with whatever we are feeling. In this we find liberation, freedom, the truth of who we are.

Our culture operates on the belief that our human experience must be binary – negative and

positive. The truth of you resides underneath your beliefs, beneath the stories that you tell, the judgments that you make, and the perceptions of right and wrong. Under that quietly resides the authentic Essential Self, the Soulful Self.

"The truth of you resides underneath your beliefs, beneath the stories that you tell, the judgments that you make, and the perceptions of right and wrong."

17. ALWAYS BEGIN AGAIN.

Begin again, and again, and again. Every day just begin again.

One of the greatest limiting factors I have witnessed in the patients and clients with whom I have worked over the years is a developed attitude that things cannot change, that "it is always going to be this way." We can become stagnant in our thinking. Optimism can be squelched by past experience that was based upon a limited reality, which played out our limiting and confining beliefs.

We step powerfully into a greater picture for ourselves when we remember and return to a truer state, fresh like the child we once were. Engage in the delight of your learning and revealing to yourself. Begin again, begin again and again, every day, as if the most important thing for you to choose is optimism, freedom, and possibility.

It is better to feel optimism, freedom, and possibility today than to hold a grudge over yesterday's outcome. When a concern keeps repeating itself, know that there is something in it for you; you'll find great medicine in it. Embrace it all, drop in, let some part of it be serving you, revealing some greater part of yourself that until now you have been unwilling or unable to see. Invite it in. And begin again.

"Begin again, begin again and again, every day, as if the most important thing for you to choose is optimism, freedom, and possibility."

18. Choose to Love.

Know that Love is the universal solvent.

Everything dissolves in Love.

This is a law of the physical world: matter is compressed energy. If you took all of the energy in all of creation (that's a lot!) and compressed it repeatedly, eventually you would create physical form. In this process, the very first vibration generated is Love.

Love transcends everything physical. Any emotion or thought you can love into will begin to soften and dissolve. Anything you can love into will begin to take on a new meaning and sometimes even a new form in your life.

Think of your heart as a spiritual bonfire. Anything and everything that you can pull into your heart will be consumed by its flame. When you put a log on a fire, the log burns to

ash and the fire blazes bigger. This is true of your heart space.

Your loving, forgiving, compassionate, passionate heart exists for one reason: it transforms energy from one form to another. Your free will to love deeply into any situation at any moment – even if you were not loving into it until just now – is infinitely transformative. This sets you apart from every other species on the planet.

Awaken to the enormity of your power to simply choose to love.

"Your loving, forgiving, compassionate, passionate heart exists for one reason: it transforms energy from one form to another."

19. SOFTEN AND MELT.

S often in Love. You're made of it. Recognize this truth, and melt.

In your softest state, you are pliable, malleable to all circumstances, and able to manage anything. Identified as the loving, light-filled Being that you truly are, you can soften at will, secure that your very being-hood faces no threat. Recognize that you, as love and as the softened Being, are infinite.

While loving into the outer world, soften your physiology. Just melt on the inside. The moment you feel a situation drawing your energy upward in the body – creating tension in the neck and shoulders, perhaps a knot in the stomach, a lump in the throat – the moment you feel any of these energies engaging, just soften and physically melt.

Strong in the spine and soft in the body, we allow energy to move through the body as

intended. In this state, we begin to interpret everything from an entirely different dimension. An alternate version of ourselves gets to have a voice, make decisions, and build relationships through Love.

"Recognize that you, as love and as the softened Being, are infinite."

20. ACCEPT YOURSELF AS THE CREATOR OF YOUR OVERALL LIFE EXPERIENCE.

You are so magnificent that you are responsible for it all: every effort, trial, failure, victory, joy, and celebratory moment; all the wonderful things, accomplishments, the happenings that brought you to your knees, deepened your heart, and opened your eyes to beauty, love and presence. You have had a say in *all* of it, whether you knew it or not.

All of it reflects your magnitude. Often, we don't want to contemplate this. We refuse to accept responsibility for our part in the "bad" things, and we think it vain or delusional to suppose we had a significant role in the creation of the "good."

When we claim responsibility for all of it, we choose a different path, and we begin to see life from an entirely different perspective. Only then we can refine the skills we came to this planet to refine.

We want to know how to manage energy, and so we come to this world where we could interact with all manner of energies, literally anything imaginable. All the vibrations show up as props – relationships, places, and circumstances – in the spectacular interactive theatre of the universe.

Walk with one eye on the inside, and you will see who you're becoming in the midst of all those engagements. Eventually, you'll understand you're not actually becoming it, you're simply remembering who you are.

Take a moment and accept your magnificence. Accept the process of remembering. This will land you in the most glorious and empowered disposition possible in this moment.

"You have had a say in all of it, whether you knew it or not."

21. KNOW THAT THERE IS ONLY ONE THING HAPPENING HERE, AND IT IS GOOD.

Everything happening in your life is serving you. This can be difficult to accept, especially in moments of heightened or acute pain or stress.

Look back over the "worst" experiences of your past, all the way back to as far as you can remember and up until this moment. You learned, evolved, and moved closer to awakening with each experience. All life experiences serve as opportunities to awaken, to realize, actualize, and materialize yourself as a God-Source Being here in a body. That's what every one of us is doing here (and there is only One of us).

As we continue to integrate this knowing, we become more willing and even relieved to quit wasting energy trying to force change in the outside world. We can then more effectively direct this energy into the cultivation of our inner world. This opens us to an expanded, even multi-dimensional experience while we

are here. This leads ultimately to our most profound awakening, to Enlightenment.

On our various paths, we often struggle to learn how to react and respond better to what someone else is creating. There's another way: as we wake up here in this dimension, we start to see that every occurrence can serve to redirect us back within. From here, we may still engage as much as we wish in managing the life experience, and we may do so now with free will and loving detachment from the result, knowing that all is well.

There is only one thing happening here, and it is good.

"Everything happening in your life is serving you."

22. Contemplate this: There is only One of us here.

Look deeply upon someone today. Really see them.

Notice when you nod and shake hands, and even hug and exchange pleasantries perhaps half-consciously, habitually, without really being present. Then really look and listen. With an open heart and mind, listen to what people say. See them. Invite them into your energy field and enfold them in your loving presence.

You can do this with someone you don't know very well, with a co-worker you've worked beside for a long time but never really got to know. You can do this with someone dear to you, a friend you've known for years, a family member. Look upon them deeply today, and sense a new vibrational frequency of connection. You will automatically touch the vibrational frequency of oneness, of union.

If this seems too intimate or potent to practice with a person that may come to mind, remember that this other person is part of you – because there is only One of us here – and that this is happening inside you, in your heart space, in your inner core. They won't necessarily be aware of it, though on some level they may feel it.

There is only One of us here. All the pieces and parts make it look as if billions of different people exist. Yet they just represent parts of our own consciousness attempting to integrate, to unify, to get to know one another, to act as one.

Approaching life in this way, we step into unity consciousness. Breath by breath, moment by moment, we build the constitution of love on the planet.

"There is only One of us here."

23. Invite the whole of you to show up in your life experience.

It may feel as if the higher self has only a toe in the river. Therefore, we may feel a sense of incompleteness and wonder, "Am I whole? Will I be okay? Will I know what to do?" We may think we're inadequate in some way.

This is only because the whole of you has not completely shown up. As peculiar as it may sound, just invite the rest of you to drop on in, to come in and then out to the surface where it can be known. Just invite it. Then go inside and be that version of you.

Be the rest of you showing up. Approach life anew, as if you've never seen it before, as if you've just now stepped into this body and opened your eyes. Look at it with that kind of curiosity, objectivity, presence, and adventure. Invite the rest of you, and then become it.

24. EACH DAY, DREAM SOMETHING.

Every day, imagine something, dream something new for you. Do this not just with your mind, but with your body. Experience what it feels like in the body for this dream to be true. Dream something not only with your emotions, but in the viscera, in your muscles, your breath, your cells. Dance to the vibration of "this is happening."

In the quietness of your mind, in your own space, in your own time, dream something new for you. Close your eyes for 30 seconds or more at a time as you dream, and feel new circuitry of possibility building.

The truth is, you are made of infinite possibility. When you imagine an experience to be real at the cellular level, that possibility builds its own circuitry. That essence starts connecting with the central nervous system, bringing the body – which is energy – into vibrational alignment with what you create in your imagination. Dream something new today. Activate your Creatorship.

25. ANCHOR LOVE MORE DEEPLY IN THE BODY THAN EVER BEFORE.

In this moment, call up an image of something you love. You might think of a person, a pet, or a situation. Bring it before you. Now notice what you feel inside the body. Holding the image before you, turn up the volume on the feeling of love. Then, turn up the volume again. Turn up the love so much that it begins to outshine the image you're holding in your mind. Expand it even more. Fill the room with this love that you're feeling.

Now, place your hands over your heart, and press into your chest. Then bring your consciousness inside the chest, and press outward toward your hands saying inwardly, *This love is for me.*

Receive it. Recognize that:

I can create, give, and receive love all at once.

I am creator and receiver.

I am made of the Love itself.

Stay in the body, and allow it to infuse your being. In this way, you can embody Love, and anchor it more deeply than ever before.

"Anchor Love more deeply in the body than ever before."

26. Today, breathe consciously as you move.

Yoga brings together conscious movement and breath. This transforms regular exercise and movement into a tremendous integrative practice that brings your consciousness more fully into the body and the here-and-now than meditation alone.

Combine some repetitive physical movement with conscious breathing today. It can be in a workout or in something as simple as walking across a parking lot or ascending a stairway.

Any movement can become yoga when you bring your awareness fully into the body and add conscious breath. It can be something as easy as standing from a chair while inhaling, sitting back down as you exhale, and repeating. You could even remain seated, lifting your spine gently while breathing deeply into the belly while exhaling as you twist to one side, then inhaling back to center and exhaling again as you twist in the other direction. Let it be simple, and do it with love.

Bring mind, body, and breath together today.

27. Bring mind, body and spirit together today.

In addition to breathing consciously as you move, breathe consciously as you *think*.

When you notice a thought upsetting you, bring your attention to the body and notice where in the body you feel a charge. Bring your consciousness to that area of the body by contracting the muscles in and around it, squeezing gently as you breathe.

If you can, squeeze and stretch the area at the same time. Gently, lovingly, and intentionally contract and extend simultaneously – as if you were arm-wrestling someone and you kept up the effort even as they were winning. While you do this, breathe and visualize the energy of your breath moving through the area. This illuminates your tissues with loving presence.

Letting your consciousness land where you feel a charge in the body in response to a thought,

and breathing while squeezing it at the same time activates the mind-body-spirit connection. This begins to dissolve patterns in the integrative nervous system, and opens you to land more easily in a state of grace.

"Letting your consciousness land where you feel a charge in the body in response to a thought, and breathing while squeezing it at the same time activates the mind-body-spirit connection."

28. Make a small nutritional shift today.

Do you habitually reach for a food or drink that you know does not support your ideal nutritional balance? Today, choose something else.

A different choice, even a small shift sends a message to the subconscious that says *I care.* The subconscious receives this, and responds accordingly.

Today, make one new choice that you know will support you. Eat an additional piece of fruit or a vegetable, or drink additional water. Do something that shows *I am awakening, and I care enough to bring some intention to what I take in.*

29. BRING LOVING PRESENCE TO AN AREA OF RESISTANCE.

Usually, the moment we think of a troubling topic, the body slips into defensive physiology. The first thing we want to do is get away from it, so we find distractions.

In this moment, insist that you're going to sit with something you've been resisting. Find one area of resistance within – a challenging relationship; a point of defensiveness; something you've been avoiding; or a situation outside your control that you continue to push against.

Hold this item of resistance in your mind's eye. Now, squeeze the tissues at the core of your body and breathe up and down the whole central channel, from head to toe and back again. Continue this contracting and central channel breathing while focusing on the area of resistance. Send this message to the subconscious:

I'm bigger than this.

I hold the space for this.

I willingly contemplate this topic of resistance.

I am open to the gift in this.

Continue to breathe and be open. Release, and relax. Bring your Loving Presence to this resistance.

"Continue to breathe and be open. Release, and relax. Bring your Loving Presence to this resistance."

30. REMEMBER FIVE JOYFUL CHILDHOOD MEMORIES.

Recently, after an hour of walking my dogs in a snowfall, I decided to bring the furry angels back home and take a walk just for me. I couldn't remember how long it had been since I'd done that. As I walked deep into the woods, there was almost a foot of snow on the ground, and such delicious silence and stillness.

Suddenly, I remembered standing in a similar place hundreds of miles away as a child. I felt a familiar physiology come over me with awe and wonder of the trees and their silence, the snow settled on them, and the crystalline quality of the air. I recognized the trees were the same, and they emanated the same energy – like a song – that I sensed from them as a kid.

In that space, I felt so renewed and refreshed. I took off running through the woods in the snow, laughing like I was seven years old again. When I came out of the woods, a father was there with

his two children building a snowman. Seeing them, I felt a kind of euphoria rushing through my system as my inner joy-of-childhood circuits lit up.

Vibrational frequencies associated with joy from your childhood have a renewing and potentially transformative quality. You can access these energies by remembering what it was like to be a child – youthful, flexible, adventurous, and like a sponge, taking everything in – and allowing yourself to revisit and experience those sensations again.

Remember five amazing childhood memories, moments that brought you joy. They don't need to be big or dramatic, they just need to feel good. Recall what it felt like, and allow it to come into the body again in the here and now.

31. Say the words, "Yes I Am."

Next time someone asks you a question, instead of answering "Yeah," or "Uh-huh," answer with a clear *Yes*. See how that feels.

The word *Yes* invites a perception of limited reality to open to limitless possibility.
It opens the mental body to the free flow of energy constantly passing through your system.
Yes opens your circuits to infinite possibility.

When you say the words *I Am*, you step toward the center of the unified field of consciousness that is you. When you say it with loving awareness, embodiment occurs. Vibrationally, *I Am* resonates deeply, like an *Om*.

Close your eyes, breathe in the belly, and quietly state, "*Yes, I Am*." Notice the vibration it activates in the body. Breathe it in.

Vibrational tones move energy through the system. You can engage these vibrations

purposefully, intentionally, and regularly simply by saying, *"Yes, I Am."*

Breathe in *Yes, I am* every day.

Breathe out *Yes, I am* just as often.

*"When you say the words I Am,
you step toward the center
of the unified field of
consciousness that is you."*

32. Raise the arms overhead every day.

At least once a day, raise your arms above your head – in a big victory "V" shape – as if creating a vessel or a chalice for energy to flow down into the body from overhead and fill it up.

When you get up each day, press your feet into the floor as you stand up, and rise for a morning stretch. Allow the arms to rise overhead while you stand, and breathe deeply, up and down through the body. Allow the sensation of energy dropping in to fill the vessel.

33. Start to create a relationship with the invisible.

Start to create a relationship with the invisible by taking action on a fly-by thought today. When a fleeting impression comes through your mind, catch it. Connect with that person who just popped into your mind. Pick up that book you suddenly remembered wanting to read. Follow that subtle impulse you just felt to look into something new that interests you.

While thoughts and impressions may seem to emerge from nowhere, they offer you opportunities. Act on a few of these ideas (the ones that feel good, and maybe even one that scares you just a little) and you start to build a relationship between the conscious and the subconscious mind. You begin a habit of listening. You demonstrate your openness to possibility. And you welcome the deep wisdom attempting to rise from within that rewires the circuitry of the protective personality to serve the joyful expansion of your consciousness.

34. Ask a question you've been avoiding.

Respectfully ask someone a question you've been afraid to ask. Set your intention to be present, to listen, and not reply immediately. When they finish responding to your question, simply say, "Thank you. I've been wanting to ask. I'll think about what you've said."

If you feel a response is appropriate and do not know what to say, just say so: "I do not know what to say. When I do, I will share. But I wanted to hear you. I wanted to give you the opportunity to share with me what you've been feeling."

Doing this allows us to shine light on fears we've kept contained. We recognize through the experience that we're capable of managing these kinds of conversations with love, compassion, vulnerably, and humility.

Ask what you've wanted to but have been afraid to ask. Be present, ask, lean in, and listen.

35. Read or listen to something inspiring every day.

Inspiring words activate an uplifting vibrational frequency in us. Make it a habit to see and hear something inspirational each day. Not only does this energize us, motivate us, and elicit joy, it also assists us to welcome energies we've been afraid of, allowing them to rise to the surface and into the light where they can be integrated.

Even if only a few sentences or for a few minutes, read or listen to something inspiring every day.

"Inspiring words activate an uplifting vibrational frequency in us."

36. Check in with your body often each day.

Often, our perspective gets fragmented. We think we are the mind; we think of ourselves as a body; or we identify as a mind that "has" a body. In reality, we are the breath. *You are the breath.* By simply directing the mind to bring attention to the body and observe what is happening between them, you begin to unify them. Your consciousness, your loving breath, is the catalyst.

Several times a day, notice what sensations you feel in the body.

How is the energy flowing here?

Am I breathing? Have I been holding my breath?

What sensations are present?

Am I allowing this body to be all that it is?

What is the body communicating to the mind?

Bring your consciousness to the energy in the body. Bring your loving attention to it by squeezing and releasing, and moving the energy through different areas.

Check in with your body several times every day. Notice what it feels, senses and says. Notice.

"By simply directing the mind to bring attention to the body and observe what is happening between them, you begin to unify them."

37. Vow to tell a victim story no more than three times.

Angeles Arrien, the late cultural anthropologist and a dear friend of mine, encountered an indigenous people with a fascinating tribal rule for living in peace, harmony, strength and vitality. Recognizing the temptation to get caught up in the past, the tribe agreed upon a rule to help them remain present.

Their rule was that one could tell a story from the position of victim – from the point of view of how hard it was to deal with, difficult to process, impossible to understand – only three times. After that, they must choose only to tell the story from a place of wisdom and reflection upon what it taught them. The consequence for clinging to victimhood by repeating the victim story beyond three times was ejection from the tribe.

Would you still be welcome in your tribe if this were the rule? Do you hold onto your stories and continue to re-tell and relive them from a victim perspective?

When you feel hurt, acknowledge it. Allow it, and have what you have. Lean compassionately into it, breathe love through it, and tell your painful story if you must. Yet vow to tell a victim version only three times. Choose those times wisely, then do not dwell there. Look for the point. Every story offers an opportunity for the revelation of wisdom.

*"Look for the point.
Every story offers an opportunity
for the revelation of wisdom."*

38. Embrace "Both/And"

The mind sees a land of duality full of Either/Or-ness. Sometimes we have difficulty making decisions because we are used to eliminating options, while our truer nature *gathers* options. The mind seeks to make distinctions and identify separateness. The heart unifies. The mind asks, "What makes this different from that?" The heart asks, "How do this and that belong here?"

If you're having difficulty making a decision, perhaps neither this nor that is your answer – it may well be *Both/And*.

How do you and I both engage and receive what we want?

I'm drawn to both these options — how can they coexist?

How do you and I proceed and create something together?

Chances are, what will serve best will be some of these *and* some of those. Be creative. It's your true nature. Mix it up. Begin to think in terms of *Both/And*. From here, we stand in a grand neutrality from which we can more easily respond from the truth of who we are.

"If you're having difficulty making a decision, perhaps neither this nor that is your answer — it may well be Both/And."

39. Choose simplicity.

Find simplicity in all things. Look for the simplest interpretation.

When I began my practice almost 30 years ago, "fun, simple, and easy" naturally came out of me as a mantra, a choice, a rule of thumb. Almost overnight, I built a thriving practice serving and helping people. Every joyful, fulfilling, and sustaining business decision I ever made came from the foundation of that intention: fun, simple and easy. I discovered that when things became more complex, they also became less fun and less sustainable.

Nature is actually quite simple and straightforward with nothing hidden, no ulterior motives. You get the lightning when it comes. You get the sunshine when it comes. It's pretty simple. Fun, simple and easy. Choose simplicity.

40. SLOW YOUR BREATH TODAY.

I once had a deeply transformative experience of awakening to my higher self during a meditation. Suddenly, in light so bright – ten times brighter than the brightest day in the desert – I could see 360 degrees around me. Beneath me, the planet Earth looked about the size of a marble, and I was embedded into it up to what would have been my knees. With each breath in, I sensed, saw, and knew this light, this brilliant bright light, was coming down through my system, way down into the Earth, as Love. I found that the more slowly and deeply I breathed, the richer, the more intense, more piercing and available Love became. I knew I was breathing Love into the planet, and I experienced a deep knowing that *this is why we are here*.

We are here to learn how to breathe, no matter what. We are here to breathe love into our earthly experiences. The more consistently we can do this, the more we uplevel the

bandwidth of human consciousness and our own experience. We soften. We embody the Love and the Light that we truly are.

If you slowly breathe in and slowly breathe out, you will automatically bring the rhythm of your system closer to your true natural state. It may not at first feel like a familiar state, but it is your natural state.

Start where you are, then practice slowing your breath. Breathe in to a count of six and exhale to a count of six. Over time, you may slow it to ten or twelve, or beyond. The slower the better. Consciously slowing your breath can be profoundly transformative for your life. Try it first in a relaxed place. Then breathe consciously during some activity that engages the right and left brain. And ultimately, practice slowing your breath when you experience stress.

Slowing your breath sets you up to to see more easily through the veil, the illusion, the *maya* of this outer world. The breath is a gateway to the truth of who you are.

41. PRACTICE COLLECTING ENERGY.

Engage in a fun and spiritual ritual of saving a dollar a day, consciously. (Because the word "save" can suggest a sense of protection, of preservation, or "keeping safe," I want to be clear that the intent here is to "collect" or "gather.") Collect some currency, and let it be fun. Do it physically. Maybe make an altar out of a little piggy bank, and play with it in this way.

This exercise isn't about the material wealth. It's about the materialization of your spiritual wealth, your abundance, your whole self. Practice honoring the collection of energy, and let it represent a quickening of energy in your life.

Culturally and societally, we bestow tremendous power upon money, and we can use this to our vibrational advantage. Money is just a concept, an energy. Its role and importance in our societies undeniably demonstrates how powerfully something manifests in the physical

world when human consciousness collectively embraces an idea.

Literally experience yourself putting money in a jar, in a box, or in a little bank – and infuse each deposit with love, as well. Consciously engage in collecting this energy, nurturing it, honoring it, and treating it as sacred. Collect some money with the sincere and playful intention that it reflect a quickening, a coming to life of your cosmic spiritual being expressing through your body.

"Practice honoring the collection of energy, and let it represent a quickening of energy in your life."

42. Buy less, and give away more.

Allow the motion in your life – the flow of energy through your space – to return to its natural balance. Open the closets in your house. Look into your storage spaces, and give away the things you do not use. Allow more space for the energy to flow through, and at the same time offer it up to someone in need.

Buy less, give away more, and celebrate the sacred space this opens up. In the freedom of this sacred space, with fewer distractions to pull our attention elsewhere, we can relax into a greater experience of the heart, relaxing into the truth of our being. We can experience balance and harmony in both our outer and inner world.

43. WALK WITH A CANDLE.

S ometime in the next few days, light a candle and walk with it across the room. As you move, notice that when you proceed with awareness and intention, the candle burns unwaveringly, steadily. Notice how you feel in your body. This beautiful exercise demonstrates a vibrational experience available to you.

Bring this quality of awareness and intention to your body as you move about your day. This is not about the speed with which you go about your activities, it is about your *presence* inside the body throughout your day. Your awareness and intention can help you – no matter how quickly you may choose to move about – to experience the unwavering steadiness of the candle flame. Know that with practice, this is how you can feel on the inside, no matter what you choose engage with in the outside world.

44. EXPAND YOUR AWARENESS.

Just as you have begun to pay attention to what's happening inside the body, bring awareness to what is happening just overhead.

The chakra system has long been measured, and has been scientifically proven. And while many of us have heard of the chakras representing seven energy centers in the body, there is more to discover. Just above your head at approximately an arm's reach, another energy center, the eighth chakra, resides. Also known as the Soul Star or North Star, this area vibrationally corresponds with life purpose and the expression of the Higher Self in the physical dimension.

When contemplating your life purpose – *What is in store for me? What calls to me next?* – engage your core muscles in the body, and allow your attention to come up above your head to the eighth chakra as you breathe through that space and the central channel of the body.

Invite your consciousness to fill the whole of your physical being and a little beyond, and you can become more adept at allowing things to materialize in your life experience. At the same time, you expand your awareness further into the truth of who you are.

"Just as you have begun to pay attention to what's happening inside the body, bring awareness to what is happening just overhead."

45. BECOME AN INSTRUMENT OF PEACE.

B̲e the channel through which peace arises.

Be the way peace shows up in every situation.

Invite others into peace with you. Be the vibration of peace. Speak into it. Instead of retaliating in an argument or a discussion, rather than fighting to be heard, to make your point, or to be right, just choose peace.

"Invite others into peace with you. Be the vibration of peace. Speak into it."

46. Remember what you're made of.

We are a flowing stream of energy, and we are here to become conscious of this. We are here to awaken to the massive creative power that we are: God-Source Energy in a body. It serves us to remember this when we get tangled up in the details of life. All we need to do is return to center, to go with this flow.

Remember that energy runs continuously through your body through an organized pathway. Energy runs through the body from high overhead as pure white light, pure energy so subtle that most barely experience it. It drops straight down through the body, through the center of the brain, the center of the throat, the center of the chest, the center of the heart and the belly, the center of the tip of the spine, and right down the legs into the earth. It is stepped down and transduced in the earth, from which it rises up again.

As it rises through the legs, through the tip of the spine, up through the belly, the heart and the throat, into the center of the brain, up and out

the top the head, it activates various components of our wholeness, of our personhood. Then, it shoots out the top of the head and cascades in every direction back toward the earth.

It comes in again at the base of the spine, and moves back up through the entire body and out the crown again, and cycles around outside the body and back in at the tip of the spine, over and over and over.

We're constantly replenished by more energy in this way. As we land our attention on this flow, we can actually support and enhance it with our consciousness. We can land our awareness on this and feel it. Doing so serves our collective awakening.

Help lead the way by cultivating this awareness within yourself. Let it dissolve tension from the body as you melt into the energy that flows through you, that you are made of. Breathe slowly, and catch a ride on this energy flowing through the body. Ultimately, recognize you *are* that energy.

47. Observe nature.

Watch nature. Be fully present with it.

While you witness the vibration of the beauty, the awe, and the wonder, it activates the same vibration within you. Notice this in the body.

When you take a walk in nature, you are taking a walk in yourself. In your moments of observation, recognize that you are part of this nature. You *are* nature. You are observing yourself, a reflection of you. Feel in your body the vibrational match of what you're experiencing on the outside. This dissolves the illusion of separation.

"Feel in your body the vibrational match of what you're experiencing on the outside. This dissolves the illusion of separation."

48. Appreciate that contraction can serve your expansion.

Have you ever found yourself thinking, *Just when I was getting it together, just as things were unfolding so beautifully, this thing came along and knocked me down?* Next time you find yourself experiencing what feels like a set-back, recognize it as a contraction intended to serve your expansion. The truth is all of creation is expanding, and that means you are too – whether you're awake to it or not. Contractions, where they occur, serve that expansion.

Consider how certain jellyfish swim through water. The creature contracts and propels itself through the water, and as this forward movement slows the jellyfish opens and expands again, and another contraction nudges it through the water once more. A dance of graceful, gentle contraction and expansion continues. We can see this dynamic of expansion and contraction at play in our life experience as well.

In a moment of contraction, realize that it isn't a problem. You might feel it as a dense vibration or a "negative" emotion, a heavy sensation, perhaps a feeling of depression, all of which are part of the big picture. Every time your life goes through a big expansion, you may notice a contraction as you integrate and anchor the expansion. Remember that both are equally necessary.

Notice when you resist an anchoring or an expansion, then consciously shift. In the joy of an expansion and in awareness of a contraction, take it to the body and breathe it into the cells. Breath through the central channel, letting it land in you where you will integrate and embody it.

Life constantly supports expansion and contraction – everything in its own right time. Recognize contraction in your life as merely anchoring on the way to greater expansion.

49. Know that all roads lead to Love.

All roads, all experiences lead to Love. If you were to write down the experiences of your life – the defining moments – and then list the things you learned and realized through those experiences, you would find a common denominator. Ultimately, all have led you toward Love. You may not have known it at the time, especially in painful experiences such as loss or heartbreak. Yet Love has always been the final destination.

Knowing that all roads lead eventually to Love helps open our eyes to read the signs along the way. This can save a lot of time as we process and integrate our life experiences. Trust and know that all roads lead to Love.

"Trust and know that all roads lead to Love."

50. Breathe Love into your brain.

Accelerate enlightenment and embodiment by awakening and illuminating the high creative centers of the brain.

The brain functions most powerfully when we allow it to work in collaborative alignment with the whole foundational system below it in the body. We can nurture this strong foundation by opening the channels of the whole system. Breathe your loving consciousness through the body as you allow an opening in the throat, the chest, the mid-belly, solar plexus, down below the navel, and through the tip of the spine, our very rootedness. This best empowers the high brain centers to perceive our infinite possibility, to function more closely with the truth of who we are, to serve our highest purpose.

Breathing low in the body and through the central channel, bring your attention up and breathe love deep into the center of the brain as well. Love into the tissues here where you

experience thoughts. By breathing Light and Love through this space in the center-front to the back, and the center, and side to side in the brain, you more fully awaken your consciousness there. This initiates the growth of new circuits for creatorship as you more fully embody the God-Source Creative Energy that you are.

"Accelerate enlightenment and embodiment by awakening and illuminating the high creative centers of the brain."

51. Stay true to this: You are Love.

L ead from the heart. Lead with your Love. When you find yourself doing otherwise, return to center.

Allow your awareness of Love as the ultimate truth to infuse your life.

"Allow your awareness of Love as the ultimate truth to infuse your life."

52. LET YOUR AUTHENTIC SELF LEAD.

K now that you are an expression of the Divine. From a place of Love, let the needs and desires of your Authentic Self express your holiness.

When you operate as your Authentic Self, destiny unfolds. When we disregard the heart in an attempt to do the "right thing" or what we think is expected of us, we move away from our authenticity, making it more difficult to experience our true magnificence.

"When you operate as your Authentic Self, destiny unfolds."

53. Remember who you are.

Quiet yourself regularly, and remember who you are. Remember you are the Essential Self. The real you resides at the core of your being. You are not a personality – you *have* a personality. When we operate through it consciously, it is the engaging personality. When we function through it unconsciously, it is the protective personality.

As we learn to quiet ourselves and re-identify as the Essential Self at the core of our being, our perspective shifts to behind the scenes. From this perspective, knowing we are divine-human holy presence, we can engage the personality to exercise free will. Here we get to observe the theatrics of the world at play, and consciously decide to what degree and with which energetic quality to participate.

As the Essential Self, we need hide from nothing. Resting in truth, we need no protection. We recognize that everything points toward the unfoldment of our magnificence.

54. Trust your gut.

Go with your gut impressions more often. This immediate impression of something is based upon billions of bits of information – exponentially more than the rational mind can even begin to entertain. When we second-guess, we begin to filter out the wisdom attempting to rise from within, and become less and less in touch with it.

Simply note the source of your impression if you feel unsure. Does it emerge from the head... or from the core? While you can trust *some* of what comes from the head, you can *always* trust what comes from the core, from your gut.

Your gut impressions represent your inner wisdom. From deep in your belly and the root of your being, you know more than you can think. Trust it. You know.

"Your gut impressions represent your inner wisdom."

55. SEE YOUR WHOLENESS.

Here's an invitation: stop looking at yourself as wounded or damaged. Likewise, lay that down about other people too. See the great unfoldment reflecting everything as an evolutionary process. This process is happening within you.

The more we allow ourselves to walk with one eye on the inside and see that we are whole and complete, that we're here simply engaging, refining, and polishing ourselves in various ways, the sooner we begin to recognize there is nothing broken and nothing wrong.

Stop trying to identify fault, damage, or weakness in yourself and in those around you. Look for the beauty and the magnificence being reflected everywhere. See yourself and others through the lens of the heart.

56. EXERCISE THE FREE WILL USE OF LOVE AT YOUR COMMAND.

Want to "win?" Recognize that Love is *the* ultimate divine power. Choose to Love in the middle of a fight and the glory of all creation floods through you. Choose to Love in the middle of a disagreement – surrender in Love. Doing this builds circuitry for Love. When we stand firmly in Love, we consciously engage our creatorship.

Love is the most magnificent tool you have. Will you choose to Love in the middle of a disagreement? Will you choose to lay it down and put Love above winning? Will you choose to make Love more important than being right? While it might seem disempowering to the mind or the ego, a choice for Love represents the highest and most empowered choice you could ever make. Ultimately when you choose Love, everyone wins. There is nothing in this dimension, on this planet, that serves you more than the free will use of Love at your command.

57. Enhance your awareness of the Thinking You and the Timeless You

Enhance your self-knowledge by bringing your attention within and sensing how you feel. Then trust this guidance and move forward. In this way, you will build a beautiful relationship between the *timeless* you and the *thinking* you. Space and time limit the thinking you, while the timeless you is bountiful and eternal. When we build a better relationship between them, the mind comes to know and trust the true, deep, Eternal Self. This empowers choices and action based in peace, love, and wholeness.

"Space and time limit the thinking you, while the timeless you is bountiful and eternal."

58. DRAW YOUR SENSES WITHIN — AND EXPAND YOUR SENSORY REACH WITHOUT.

Know that the real you resides deep within the core of your own physical being. You can direct your awareness to see it within and feel it with your senses. As you build this awareness at the deep, physical core of your body, more of you awakens as you land in the body *as* consciousness, and this laser-focusing raises your vibration through the column of your inner core.

Aligning and energizing this column of conscious awareness leads to the illumination of the inner eye, which literally allows you to sense and see various and multiple realms of your being. With access to these realms, you can step forward with deep wisdom.

Look in, reach in, and breathe into the core of your body as if looking down a well filled with pure white light. Look down through the central channel of the body. As we build this familiarity,

the vibrational frequency of the inner core begins to rise. This eventually illuminates the high brain centers and allows us to sense and feel far beyond the five senses.

"Know that the real you resides deep within the core of your own physical being."

59. SEE WITH YOUR HEART.

When my mother passed, I began finding four-leaf clovers. She and I shared an affinity of and experience with four-leaf clovers, so they were very special to me. Finding them after her passing felt significant. We often see this kind of happening as evidence of a sign from someone on the other side. I assure you that from the other side, signs are constantly provided. The question is, are we tuned in to the signs being offered? Can we catch them?

I began finding four-leaf clovers because I was seeing with my heart. I felt so broken and sad, missing her at the time, that I certainly wouldn't have called it an open door. It felt like a door had closed. But I knew a door to the inner world was opening, and with the purity of the vision this opening brought with it, I found so many four-leaf clovers. Every time I turned around I found more, hundreds, and with them, unmistakably and palpably, my mother's loving, joyful presence.

After I shared my four-leaf clover find with some friends, some neighborhood children knocked on my door, asking if I was the "the clover lady." I invited them into the backyard and showed them how to find four-leaf clovers. They looked, but couldn't see them. I said, "You're looking with your eyes. You have to look with your heart." As I did so, I pointed to the ground and right there would be a four-leaf clover. I would pick it, and their eyes would grow big, their mouths dropped open, and we would giggle. Then they began finding them, too, because they knew what to do.

When we see with our hearts, we can see through the dimensions... See with your heart.

"When we see with our hearts,
we can see through the dimensions...
See with your heart."

60. APPRECIATE THE DISTINCTION BETWEEN BELIEF AND TRUTH.

Appreciate the distinction between belief and truth, and unplug from your beliefs as often as possible. Consider that your beliefs may be untrue. Most beliefs are untrue on some level inasmuch as they emerge from stories, and all can limit us in one way or another. Speak into life as if there were no limitation, the way you would if you were infinitely free.

When you hear yourself speaking something as though it is a truth, check in and see if perhaps it's only a belief. When we become willing to do this, when it becomes our practice, we rise above the limits we accepted along with our beliefs.

"Speak into life as if there were no limitation, the way you would if you were infinitely free."

61. CHECK YOUR IDENTIFYING DESCRIPTIONS.

Notice how you describe yourself. "I am a cancer survivor." "I am a Christian." "I am a Jew." "I am shy." "I am this ... or that." Each of these statements (especially with the powerful "I Am") casts us into a story-context defined by beliefs and interpretations of experiences. This creates, re-creates, and reinforces a limited reality, as if placing us in a box of our own design.

Any time we have an identification bound in something we have already been through, or something that has just been handed to us, we operate more in survivorship than creatorship without even knowing it. Begin to notice when you allow yourself to be plugged into and categorized by some half-awake, half-free system. You are here for so much more than that.

Notice your identifiers. When someone asks who you are, what you do, or what's going on

with you, be very clear. Next time, speak from your creatorship. Find an ingenious way to describe your engagements on this planet, and be conscious of what follows "I Am."

Here are a few to get you started:

"I am healthy."

"I am exploring..."

"I am opening to..."

"I am loving..."

"I am discovering..."

"Find an ingenious way to describe your engagements on this planet, and be conscious of what follows 'I Am.'"

62. Recognize that all emotions serve.

In truth, there are no good or bad emotions. They are all just vibrational frequencies. High-frequency emotions such as joy, bliss, and elation expand us. Low-frequency emotions, like sadness, grief, and remorse anchor us. All these energies serve the great pulsation of your overall expansion. Although expansion is inevitable – it's why we're here – we can slow it down in time. By denying or rejecting certain emotions, we temporarily arrest our expansion.

All emotions are here for you. The soul wants the full keyboard experience – to experience every note in the energetic symphony – and it does not have prejudice. When we deny and reject an emotion, it hovers in the energy field around the physical body, constantly clouding our life experience. To shift this, we must begin embracing all emotional states. There is nothing wrong with any of them. Do not allow the thinking mind to limit the soul's experience.

You metabolize and integrate an emotional state by embracing it, so have what you have. There is no need (and it is often preferable not) to act upon it. As loving awareness, lean into the emotional energy. Only then can it transform into something else.

"Do not allow the thinking mind to limit the soul's experience. You metabolize and integrate an emotional state by embracing it, so have what you have."

63. Don't burden yourself with judgment — especially your own.

Allow yourself to see without judgment, not because it makes you a good person but because it allows you to continue to be free in your natural state. The next time you find yourself describing something judgmentally, reframe it. Stop mid-sentence if you can, or follow it with another sentence from your loving consciousness: "Wow, I really don't mean that. I heard myself say it, and I'm interested in shifting that perception." When you do this out loud, you model it for others. Awaken out loud. Set yourself free from judgment. As soon as you recognize it in yourself, shape-shift it and see how you feel.

64. DWELL IN LOVE.

Simply sit in Love.

108 times a day, simply find a way to love.

65. Remember you are Spirit breathing spirit into the physical dimension.

Remember, YOU are Breath breathing itself, just as you are Life living itself and Love loving itself. You are the Oneness of it all.

Breath is spirit. YOU are spirit. You are Breath breathing itself, as Spirit in a body. We are all Spirit breathing itself and working out the billions of ways this consciousness can awaken to Love. That's all we're doing. We're living Love. The sooner we can remember that in every situation, the sooner we will experience divinity and unity in this collective human experience.

"You are Breath breathing itself, as Spirit in a body."

66. Intentionally create sacred space inside the body.

Ever had a deliciously great, satisfying morning stretch where every cell in your body seemed to be squeezing and stretching at the same time? Your body craves this automatic reset every day, and you can recreate it frequently.

Stretch open the inside of your body every day. Create sacred space. When you're enjoying your morning stretch, bring your consciousness fully in the body and stretch from the inside out. By doing this, you create sacred space inside the body.

Create sacred space inside the body and know, *this is where I live*. Be inside the body and feel it as you bend to each side, stretch out, and open up. Continue to do the same with your neck and your whole body, your lower back, your belly, all of it. Create awareness in the inner sanctum of your physical being. Be fully here.

67. Identify as the Essential Self first thing — before your feet hit the floor.

Before your feet hit the floor in the morning, identify as the Essential Self at your core. Be in this awareness as your feet hit the floor and decide: *This day belongs to me. I choose what thoughts get created. I choose the physiology I carry in my body. I choose the amount of joy I experience, regardless of my external environment.* As you wake each day, identify as the eternal being here to have an amazing Soulful experience.

"Before your feet hit the floor in the morning, identify as the Essential Self at your core."

68. CREATE A SACRED SPACE IN YOUR LIVING SPACE.

Create an altar in your home, a sacred space in your living space. Select objects for it that remind you of your divinity. Consider a yoga mat for the space that you can step onto each day, sit, stretch, and breathe consciously. Create sacred space in your life that you cannot miss. And let it be fun.

When you have an altar in your home, your physiology changes every time you walk by it. The more you change your disposition when you pass by this altar, the more the altar holds the energy for you. It can become a powerful reminder and a compelling invitation for you to pause and bring your awareness back to the core when you find yourself in an unconscious state.

69. REMEMBER A TIME WHEN YOU KNEW THAT YOU KNEW.

Remember a time when you knew that you knew? Honor that. Take it to the body. Allow yourself to feel and breathe the presence of that knowing. Build that vibrational frequency at the cellular level, and remember it often. In this way, we build a soulful constitution that allows us to traverse life with grace and ease and the power of our deep wisdom.

70. Know that your greatest challenges are polishing you.

Your biggest challenges are polishing your greatest attribute. You're finding ways to make the mind let your soul out. You're finding ways to let yourself reveal. Reframe the way your mind sees your challenges. Accept that they serve you, that you even requested them in your life so that you could polish yourself against them. Your mind comes to know the truth of who you are when it lets go of story and victimization, and rather sees challenges as completely here to help it find the greatest you, the real you.

"Reframe the way your mind sees your challenges."

71. OBSERVE YOUR MIND CHATTER AND KNOW IT'S NOT YOU.

It happens as you drive your car, as you weed the garden, as you walk the dog, as you do the dishes. It happens as you make the bed, when you're in the shower... the mind chatter runs all the time. Observe it and recognize that it's not you.

The chatter is a product of the mind. The mind isn't you, either. The mind is a tool you have, that you carry always, and that rarely shuts off. Imagine if you were carrying around a power tool all the time that was running constantly! You'd take care to be conscious of what it was up to, wouldn't you?

Just observe the chatter of the mind, and quietly breathe love into it. When you begin to breathe in observation of your mind, the chatter slows. Excessive mind-chatter represents dispersed, unfocused energy, so the more the mind chatters, the less present you are. As soon as you bring consciousness to it, you become more present.

72. Extend your meditation time.

If you're not meditating at all, 10 minutes a day is a simple place to start. When this becomes comfortable, you can increase the time. If you are already meditating for 10 minutes per day, make it 20. Extend your meditation time.

Find a mantra to repeat if you have a difficult time sitting for 20 minutes. Repeat this mantra over and over. You may find times that the mind goes still and suddenly you realize you're not saying the mantra. Simply begin repeating it again without judgment. This is exactly right on course.

This is how we train the mind to know that you – not the mind – are in charge. Remember, the essential true Beingness that is you *has* a mind. You have a mind, but the mind is not the whole you, and it is not in charge.

Choose a mantra. It could be *God*. It could be *Om*. It could be anything that opens your body,

your throat, and your heart. Choose a mantra that feels good to repeat, and put the mind to work on repeating it in meditation – the mind insists on working all the time anyhow, right? Allow the mantra to soothe the mind enough to slow down; so that you can disconnect your identity from the mind. As that begins to happen, you awaken within.

"You have a mind,
but the mind is not the whole you,
and it is not in charge."

73. See new soul friends everywhere.

When you meet someone, see them as a potential soul friend. Look at everyone, strangers too, as playing roles in order for you to find your true magnificence.

When you make a new acquaintance and you reach out to shake a hand or extend your arms for a hug, recognize in that moment the potential for a new soul connection. Think, *This is my friend.*

Approached this way, life responds accordingly. All of life responds to your intentionality. It has no choice but to do so. The more lovingly focused you are in your central core, the more powerfully you generate an external life reflecting this back to you. See new soul friends everywhere.

74. See us all on the same team.

Just as you can see individual new acquaintances as soul friends, apply this to groups as well. When you walk into a room full of people you don't know, see them as friends. See the entire crowd as your team, whether they ever become aware of it or not. It's actually the truth, because we *are* all here in collaboration. When you land your consciousness in this realization and let it anchor in the core of the body, it becomes electromagnetic and magnified. We are collaborating with the wholeness of creation as a means for it to express, through us, into this physical dimension. Bringing the light to the density. Bringing high frequency energy here. Bringing heaven on earth.

75. See someone from their mother's eyes.

Often we try to point out what a person could be doing differently to make their – or our own – lives better. We take our judgments and assessments as fact, and proceed in our relationships accordingly. This practice steals our energy and robs us of divine relationships with each other.

Think of someone with whom you have something unresolved, and choose to see them through their mother's eyes. See the beauty and the perfection in them. See them as the child they once were, and consider how their mother would have looked at them. Think of how God sees them. Recognize their potential, wanting to come out. See them through their own mother's eyes, when they were young and innocent and pure and full of potential. Let your mind linger for a while in this loving perception, and explore its implications.

76. BREATHE HIGH FREQUENCY PURE WHITE LIGHT THROUGH YOUR BODY.

B reathe high frequency pure white light in from overhead, down through your body, and exhale it out to two feet below where you sit or stand. Do this as often as you can.

This isn't just a mysterious practice; it's scientifically proven to be advantageous. It anchors consciousness in the body. When we practice this daily, we begin to awaken to the energy that we are. We feel better, more vital, more energetic. More importantly, we begin to cultivate our awareness as Essential Self, as essential truth pouring through the body.

77. Breathe so you can hear it.

As often as you can throughout the day, breathe so that you can hear it in the back of your throat. Squeeze the throat just a little and allow yourself to hear the breath rushing down and through. This yogic practice, called Ujjayi Breathing, helps bring you back into the body.

Be present. Be here. Bring your awareness to your breath, let yourself hear it, and allow the breath to help anchor you in the heart, in the core, and inside the body completely. This is how we begin to sense a greater version of who we are.

"As often as you can throughout the day, breathe so that you can hear it in the back of your throat."

78. PRACTICE THE FEELING OF JOY.

Notice how you feel in your body when you are happy, elated, and joyful, and memorize the pattern. Then, practice invoking that feeling with your free will. Next time you're extremely happy upon seeing someone, feeling blessed by a beautiful day, in the wonder of the beauty of the holidays, or in a deep state of joy, take one eye on the inside and memorize how it feels in your body. Then later on – in the morning when you wake, and periodically throughout the day – practice it on command. With your free will, generate more of this vibrational experience in your life.

It will become your new baseline.

79. KNOW THERE IS A RELATIONSHIP BETWEEN PHYSICAL SYMPTOMS AND REJECTING THOUGHTS.

When we reject an experience, we stop energy from flowing through the physical body in the direction that it is intending to flow. When we reject, we reverse that energy flow. With a constant state of rejection, we begin to feel it and the body begins to break down. The body and mind begin to tire.

Many of us make distinctions for ourselves regarding what works and what doesn't. Then when we witness others behaving contrary to our preferences, we put up walls of resistance and rejection both consciously and subconsciously. A beautiful practice exists for you right here in these moments: observing and allowing *what is*, without judgment. This is not to suggest we abdicate our free will – we still get to choose what we're interested in and where we want to focus our creative energy at the same time that we allow what is. We can make distinctions and have

our preferences without rejecting or judging
what unfolds.

If you're experiencing physical symptoms, this
practice can help because every physical symptom
begins with an energetic breakdown in flow,
without exception. Our rejections contribute to
that breakdown. Sometimes we reject and resist
without conscious awareness. It may even occur
in the womb. In this moment, we can begin a
practice of embracing absolutely everything
that we encounter. It is even retroactive, as the
truth of you exists beyond space and time.
You will shine.

*"In this moment, we can begin
a practice of embracing absolutely
everything that we encounter."*

80. RECOGNIZE THE CYCLE THROUGH WHICH YOUR LIFE MOVES.

Realize that the whole of your life always moves in cycles of energy. We cycle from creating to sustaining to deconstructing, then again back to creating, where we begin again. Our cycles vary in scale. Some may begin, end, and start over several times a day. Other cycles last years. Between the deconstruction phase and the beginning of something new (especially in the longer cycles), we may experience a void, a stillness. The void may feel long, and it can be as brief as a blink, and it may even overlap the creation and the birth of something new. We can struggle against the cycles, or we can with grace allow the cycles to unfold through the phases of creation, preservation, and deconstruction.

If it feels like you're having to let go of something, recognize that it represents the close of a cycle and heralds the beginning of something new. With each cycle, you spiral upward into higher vibrational frequencies as

you create something new. When it feels like you're coming around the bend into something you've been in before and you've not been in resistance to this cycle, allow yourself to know that this is a higher vibrational frequency version of whatever you're finding familiar. You are ever spiraling upward in consciousness.

"We cycle from creating to sustaining to deconstructing, then again back to creating, where we begin again."

81. Live Heaven on Earth

The ancient sacred texts – the Vedas, the Scriptures, the Upanishads, the Yoga Sutras – the oldest writings of all time (some as old as 9000 years) all direct our consciousness toward awakening. They point to the realization of the truth of who we are, and offer clues to awakening in the body to Heaven on Earth. If Heaven on Earth is here and now (as we are told), what does that mean?

Contemplate what "Heaven on Earth" means to you. Specifically, what does it feel like in the body to know this is true? Let this land in you. Feel it. Breathe it. Anchor it. And from this state, rise and take action every day.

The ancient texts have been telling us all along: It's right here. You are an integral part of the greatest story ever told continuing to unfold.

82. BREATHE INTO AND THROUGH YOUR SOLAR PLEXUS.

Your solar plexus (just below where your ribs splay apart) is energetically associated with your personal power and esteem. With your wisdom vibrating deep in your belly and your heart in the center of your chest, the solar plexus – the energetic center of your personal power – resides between them. Learn to breathe into this area to help bring and keep these energies alive.

Bridge your wisdom and your love with your own acceptance of "me too." Allow yourself to think and know:

I get to be included in the equation.

I get to make choices that benefit me, too.

When I include myself, when I ultimately allow this to be true, I am better empowered to serve. I am in my power, which gives me the ability to stand in truth for myself and others.

Breathe in your solar plexus more often, and experience your personal power.

83. Show Up, Pay Attention, Tell the Truth, and Let Go

A friend and mentor of mine, Angeles Arrien, who recently passed, spoke about four important things as a way of living:

1. Show up.
2. Pay attention.
3. Tell the truth.
4. Let go.

In honor of her, I'd like to expound a little.

To *show up* to life, engage. Find the constitution in your inner core, and breathe some life into it. "Lean in" to things about which you find yourself procrastinating. Show up.

Pay attention to what really matters. Are you getting involved in dramas that don't really matter? Are you ignoring some things that do? Pay attention to what has heart and meaning to you, not to what is dramatic.

Tell the truth. Speak your truth with great courage, and speak it sooner than you would have in the past. When you let it out, you let your soul reveal, and allow life to unfold the way it's meant to unfold for you.

Let go of the outcome. Let go of how you think it's supposed to look. The experience you desire will happen more readily as you let go of the expectation of how it's supposed to present itself.

Be focused on the internal sensation that you feel when you show up, and pay attention to what has heart and meaning. Then speak your truth and be free. Let go of everything else. Nothing else matters, it just slows down the process. You cannot do this wrong, you can only do it long. If you find it difficult to let go, it is because you haven't done one of the other three.

Thank you, Dr. Angeles, for all that you brought to the planet.

84. Be aware of your perceptions.

Our beliefs and the degree to which we are awake determines our perceptions. When we see life from a place of victimization, we get to have that experience. When we see that anything is possible, we get to have that experience. What we perceive as true becomes our reality.

The invitation here is to elevate and expand your perception. Still the mind, and be more observant. Soften the stronghold that beliefs have on your system by noticing and recognizing them as only that: beliefs.

Beliefs are just thoughts you've had for a long time. Nothing more.

Meanwhile watch, sense, and feel people on the outside. Watch, look, sense, and feel the energy of you, your true spirit, on the inside. Perceive as spirit. Allow your awareness to increase. Instead of having to be the one that speaks, be

quiet and listen. Breathe in your belly, and rest in stillness as you observe. This elevates and expands your perception, and allows you to perceive with clearer wisdom.

See what really needs to be said and what doesn't. You'll know.

See what really needs to be acted upon and what doesn't. You'll feel it.

"Beliefs are just thoughts you've had for a long time. Nothing more."

85. Recognize friction in your life as spirit coming into form.

When high frequency energy Spirit hits more dense energy, friction occurs. Live noticing your inner world and know that all friction in your life is simply spirit coming into form. If you allow yourself to feel the friction, you don't need to do the drama and the story writing. It is as simple as that.

Friction looks like a challenge with your in-laws; with your teenagers; with your boss; with your body; with your own mind. And yet it is merely spirit coming into the physical dimension. When we're aware of this, we can work with it consciously. When we're unaware, we deflect it out into a story in an attempt to give it meaning. Then we think the story gave rise to the friction although it occurred the other way around.

When you experience friction, stay centered in the core of your being. Relinquish judgment, have what you have, and breathe love through it. Recognize friction in your life as spirit coming into form. More of *you* is coming to the party.

86. ENGAGE IN RIGOROUS EXERCISE MORE THAN ONCE EVERY WEEK.

Getting your heart rate up increases endorphins and promotes cardiovascular health. I expect this is not news to you. I offer it as a reminder that it isn't enough to just think more positively. To make it real, we have to bring it into the physical dimension, bring it to the body. We can do this by engaging the body rigorously.

Breathe and move. Bring the heart rate up. Allow your respiration to increase in intensity so much that you have to really concentrate on your breath. Do this for 30 minutes as close to daily as possible. This brings the body into service as an active participant in the big picture of your life. It raises the body's vibrational frequency, and helps the mind, body, and breath to connect more readily.

If you have avoided exercise in the past, know that this is an act of love for yourself. Be creative. There are many ways to move, so find one that you can enjoy, and engage in rigorous exercise. Do this at least twice a week, and every day if possible.

87. One, two, or three days a week (or more), eat vegetarian.

This is a big one for some: perhaps one, two or three days a week, eat vegetarian. When you eat a vegetarian diet, your vibration will increase. When you raise your vibrational frequency, you will transform your life. You will alkalize the body to a greater degree, and will increase the frequencies your mind can tap into. The higher the vibrational frequency of your system, the higher the vibration your thoughts can reach. It is directly proportional. Your body will thank you. Please give it a try.

"When you eat a vegetarian diet, your vibration will increase."

88. ENGAGE WITH THE AWARENESS THAT YOU ARE PART OF NATURE.

When the heart and the brain come together as we engage with the awareness that we are part of nature, the mind begins to resonate as the trees, as the grass, as the breeze. When this begins to happen, we begin to tap into another realm.

When you're walking around in life, remember this: sun to the earth, earth to the heart, heart to the brain. Your brain receives impulses, information from your heart. Your heart receives information from the earth. The earth receives information from the sun. If we can remember this connection, we will begin to engage ourselves as part of nature.

Be aware of this connection when you're walking in nature or in the park. Be awake to it when you're outside breathing so that you can memorize these frequencies when you're indoors. Trees hold amazing high-frequency

intelligence. They bridge the worlds: the upper world, the middle world, and the lower world. Leaves take in the sunlight, and through photosynthesis, the upper world. The tree trunk lives here in the middle world. And it is in their root system, in the lower world, where spirit is anchored. When walking past the tree, ask it how it does what it does, and listen. Allow the trees to answer. Allow yourself to feel its answer – a beautiful practice.

The brain receives information from the heart, the heart from the earth, the earth from the sun. Reconnect, then root yourself, and metabolize all of life as food for your nourishment and unfoldment.

**89. LET THIS WISDOM LIBERATE YOU:
IT TAKES LESS ENERGY TO ACCEPT THAN
IT DOES TO REJECT.**

I'll leave it at that. It takes less energy to accept than it does to reject.

90. Use your feeling body to move gracefully through fluctuating emotional states.

Your body communicates with you. That knot in your stomach will have to be released eventually. Notice the tightness as it is occurring, and run your breath through it. Breathe through it to resolution. This practice will serve your relationships. The moment that your body contracts, find it, feel it, and begin to breathe through it. Wake it up. In this way, we begin to use the feeling body, to engage with it consciously, and empower ourselves to move through emotional states rather than get caught up in them.

91. TAKE BIG BELLY BREATHS FREQUENTLY THROUGHOUT YOUR DAY.

The second chakra, below your navel, relates to your deep wisdom. It begs for your attention. When you have a "gut feeling," your wisdom is rising. If you take deep belly breaths and keep it awake, it will bring its wisdom to the mind's attention. Take big belly breaths all day long.

"When you have a "gut feeling," your wisdom is rising. If you take deep belly breaths and keep it awake, it will bring its wisdom to the mind's attention."

92. PRACTICE YOGA

A yoga practice will serve you tremendously. Investigate local yoga classes, which are commonly available for virtually all ages and skill levels. Practiced regularly, yoga will make you feel younger. A practice doesn't have to be difficult, and you can begin exactly where you are, regardless of your body's current state of strength and flexibility. It can begin with a simple conscious movement integrated with breath.

The mind needs to come into the body and breathe as often as possible. Mind, body, and breath have to meld together. This is the basis of yoga.

Specific to yoga as exercise, are the scared geometries yoga creates through specific poses. This moves healing energy through the body in specific and significant ways. Practice Yoga.

93. LISTEN TO YOUR BODY.

Your body runs its systems on a priority basis for survival. Your mind feeds information to the body, from which it determines whether or not it needs to be in survival mode. Sometimes the mind can cause priorities to get mixed up and out of balance. When healing does not occur automatically, this imbalance is at play.

At night when you lie in bed, ask the body to tell the mind about a pain pattern or condition. Over a few days and nights, you will receive answers. Heed them, and your life will transform. Your body will give your mind the information it needs. Let the mind connect with the body's wisdom.

"Let the mind connect with the body's wisdom."

94. Speak your truth. Listen to the truth. And take action.

In my practice, I have seen countless people with aches, pains, and stiffness in their necks and upper bodies. The throat chakra represents this area of the body. Feelings here reflect how we're doing with speaking our truth, and also how well we're listening to the truth.

If you're experiencing pain in your neck and upper body, you're receiving a message in the form of a physical challenge. For neck and shoulder issues to resolve, you must speak your truth, be willing to listen and hear the truth, and take action on the truth. It's as simple as that. When people begin to stretch and do breath work with this in mind then take action, transformation occurs. I have seen so many examples of this with patients over the last 30 years. Speak your truth with heart and meaning, listen to the truth with deep self-compassion, and take action with grace.

95. Move with Passion, Compassion, Forgiveness, and Love.

You are the creator, the bringer of the good. You are operating, co-creatively, with the great loving presence of God-source energy itself. Allow this to happen through you, and life purpose unfolds.

Soften in the heart center. Know that a fear of betrayal, codependency, blood sugar issues, high blood pressure, shallow breathing, and a sensation of melancholy are all signs that your heart chakra or heart energy is not expressing freely or flowing. It is being compressed, protected. To shift this, move with passion, compassion, forgiveness, and love.

When we keep focus on our process of awakening to our life purpose, forgiveness becomes easier. When we realize that all things in life happen to serve our awakening to our own personal power, it allows us to soften our hearts again and again. When the heart softens, heart chakra-related issues begin to resolve. Joyfully soften and melt in the heart.

96. GROUND YOURSELF.

Ground yourself in knowing that this is your life. If you are not grounded in the realization that this life is your life, your gig, that it belongs to you, or that you have a say and that you're to have it your way, then you develop an inability to be still inside. Subsequently, you develop poor general health and low vital energy. Vital force drops. You become less aware mentally, lethargic, even foggy or flighty when you are not grounded in the truth of your being.

The truth of you is that you came here to generate an experience of yourself. By acting out of fear or people-pleasing, we stymie the entire project. Ground yourself in the knowing that "this is my gig."

"Ground yourself in knowing that this is your life."

97. REMEMBER WE ARE ALL WAKING UP IN VARIOUS WAYS AT DIFFERENT TIMES.

You may be good at some things and some aspects of a project today, and less so in a month. Maybe you used to be able to do some things that you feel you aren't able to do today. Maybe today you're better at some things that you used to not be able to do at all. Have understanding and patience with the self for this journey. Refrain from judgment. Any skill-set that you previously developed but no longer wish to engage with will be put to use in the future. You'll just use it differently. All of the development that has been happening all along the way serves all of the good for all of your life. Love it all.

98. Notice your sensitivities.

We are sensory beings: we have 100 to 1,000 times more sensory fibers than motor fibers in our nervous system. We are sensitive beings, built as a sensory system. When we are not integrated, we become "sensitive" in the way that we are used to hearing that word – that is we become "over sensitive" or we take things personally.

When we're integrated, we sense without taking things personally. We notice when we're getting our feelings hurt, and we ask ourselves if there is another way, a less personal way, to look at the situation. When the personal becomes impersonal, we begin to set ourselves free. We experience ourself as the Soulful being that we are. Just think about that. If I am taking things too personally, I will experience freedom by taking them less personally. The longer I live less personally, the more I begin to come into contact with universal truths like:

There's only one thing happening here and it is good.

There's only one of us here and it is me — the soulful self, the spirit self — and I am the ever unfolding truth of God-source energy in a body.

I am here to bring love to the planet.

It is when these universal truths begin to feel *personal* that we know we are truly awakening to our Divine Self, to our Divine Presence. This is what is meant to be for us.

Notice your sensitivities, and begin to turn them into something that works for you. Is there another way, a less personal way, to interpret what is going on? Is there a more giving, more forgiving way that is kinder, without the need always to change external circumstances?

99. Cultivate timelessness in your own being.

Look over the years of your life and recall all the amazing things you have seen and experienced. Remember the players as well, those people who played roles in your experience. Know they have all been part of your grand plan, your Soulful Contracts. Know that there are many more of these contracts in place coming down the road every day.

You requested all of these experiences with all of these collaborators, and each one is divine. Now, see yourself flying overhead above them all. Imagine them waving at you, taking a bow as in a curtain call of a great play – because that is what this life has been, and what it is.

Do this regularly. The high points will tend to come to mind, and different ones will occur to you at different times. As you reflect on these experiences and see them for what they really are — a great, grand play – you cultivate timelessness.

100. Choose to accept that you may be the spiritual leader in your circle of life.

Accept that you may be a spiritual leader. As you consider this, begin to model it for others. With the thoughts you choose and the actions you take, demonstrate the frequency of Love we get to embody on the planet. Do this not to teach, but simply to live your truth. Do this with grace, compassion, and Love – without expectation and without condition. Choose to accept that you just may be a spiritual leader in your circle of life.

"With the thoughts you choose and the actions you take, demonstrate the frequency of Love we get to embody on the planet."

101. Let All Your Talents Emerge

Realize that when you landed in this life, you first developed your "A team" of talents – the things that you were naturally good at, the things that came easily to you. You developed an identity based upon those gifts and talents, and they took you so far. In order to get you farther, realize that what got you "here" won't necessarily get you "there." You may need to call upon your "B team" and even your "C team" to get where you want to go.

Lean in to the less developed parts of yourself, and recognize that even while you're developing these new talents, you can still rely on your "A team." You're just developing your "B team" right now, too. And when you're really up against something with which you feel stuck and unable to move, know that it might mean your "C team" is being called to the field. You're still highly competent with your "A team." And you're getting better with your "B team", apparently, because that's what

invited the "C team" to come off the bench and onto the playing field. Notice all your gifts and talents are still gifts and talents, and know that there are even more waiting for you to uncover them. Are you ready?!

"Notice all your gifts and talents are still gifts and talents, and know that there are even more waiting for you to uncover them."

102. Always be open and listening.

Remember that the best teachers are good students too, so do not try to have "already arrived" and know everything. One of my greatest joys between teaching my workshops is listening and learning. May we always be listening and learning, both inwardly and outwardly.

103. RECOGNIZE THE VOICE OF THE ESSENTIAL SELF.

Know that the voice of your Essential Self is declarative and directive. It sounds like: "It's time to take a vacation." "Call your sister now." "Time to let go." "You know that you know."

The Essential Self's voice never judges, criticizes or doubts. It's not made of that vibrational frequency. If these kinds of things are running through your consciousness, recognize them as coming from the Protective Personality, the False Self, and that the outer False Self is attempting to run the show. That which is meant to assist you as the driver is attempting to take the wheel. Time to stop the bus.

Stop second-guessing. Think in terms of "I know that I know, and this self-criticism isn't what I know, it's what I *think*." (Get the difference?) "What I know in my heart is that

I'm a good person, that I am here with loving intentions, and the very fact that I'm reading this type of book shows I am interested in being all that I can be."

That you are loved and loving, that you are good, *that you are goodness itself,* is exactly all you need to know – to remember. You are that. It's time to begin putting it into practice.

"That you are loved and loving, that you are good, that you are goodness itself, is exactly all you need to know — to remember."

104. Love into all emotional states and feelings.

As we are stepping into oneness consciousness, remember there is nothing you are "not supposed to" think or feel. You must allow it all in order to metabolize it all. When we try to resist anything, we step into duality. To experience oneness consciousness, embrace all of your emotional and feeling states as good, and allow them to serve. This doesn't mean acting on every impulse. It means practicing what you know: breathing consciousness and Love into and through the body wherever and whenever your feelings get your attention. In many cases, this is all the action needed.

105. Turn fear into curiosity.

It could be said a thousand times without over-emphasis: Turn fear into curiosity.

Fear is only the recognition that there is a part of you that you don't know yet – that you haven't yet remembered. If you knew all of the parts of you, you would fear nothing. If there is something that you are fearing, free yourself by turning that fear into curiosity. It may be the single most powerful thing you can do.

"If there is something that you are fearing, free yourself by turning that fear into curiosity."

106. Consciously engage in Awakening.

When we are steeped in victimization, feeling like we don't have any power or choice in our lives, we are also steeped in addiction. Besides addictions to food, drugs or alcohol, we experience addictions to perfectionism; to intensity; to the need to know; and to focusing on what's not working in the world. Move to creatorship. In this moment, where you are right now, still the mind and come home.

Is perfectionism your addiction? Focus on your personal best even if it's not "*the* best." Insistence on perfection is a no-win game, and only guaranties continued self-criticism. Excellence is more than enough.

Does intensity have a pull on you? I have worked with many people who found themselves creating dramas in their lives just when things were going well. They eventually developed the self-awareness that the jolt of adrenaline or cortisol associated with the fear-based, intense moments somehow

soothed part of them. They had become accustomed to it. If you relate to this, allow this new self-awareness to help guide your choices, and choose Love. Find a way to consistently experience Love in your life, unconditionally. Love consistently, and allow yourself to feel *that* intensity in the body.

Do you always need to know? Express from a place of wisdom, and recognize that it's also okay *not* to know. There's actually freedom in it. Allow yourself to operate with a spirit of *I'll know when I get there*. Because you will.

If you constantly look for what's wrong or what's not working, remember the big picture: you're here to wake up. From this perspective, everything is working. There is nothing that is *not* working. Shift the question, then, to *What is this working toward?* If you can maintain this big picture perspective, your whole life serves your awakening to your magnificence. Everything is working toward that – no exceptions.

107. LOVE. ALWAYS.

Never consciously withhold your Love. As soon as you see yourself doing so, stop, shift, and step through the threshold into the generosity of spirit. When we withhold our Love trying to teach a lesson or make a point, we actually hurt ourselves. We stop the energy flow, and we affect our health. Though it may feel satisfying in some way from a lower vibrational perspective, it is simply not a good trade – nowhere near a good trade. Never consciously withhold Love. You personally transform your life experience when you step through the tendency to withhold, and Love instead.

Love. Always.

"You personally transform your life experience when you step through the tendency to withhold, and Love instead."

108. The Great Invitation: Awaken to the fact that we are already through the threshold.

We are not headed to Divinity in human consciousness; *We are here in it now.*

In my workshops, I often ask, "How many of you feel like you're on the precipice of something grand, that you're about to break through into something, or that something is about to happen?" Almost everyone raises their hand.

I marvel over this. The reason we stop at this place and feel like we're almost ready to break through is that we've not built the circuitry of realizing we are already through the threshold. We see ourselves as "almost" there, so we continue to perceive for just that: "almost there." The very words we use to describe that state depict a double layer of separation: "almost" and "there" rather than "now," "here."

This moment is not a time to try, to scrape, to scratch and crawl our way to the threshold of

Life and recognize ourselves as Divine beings. We must build the circuitry not for "almost being there" but actually for being right here in this knowing, already through the threshold.

This requires our imagination, and not in the limited way we have been used to thinking. Many of us were taught to dismiss this amazing power as insignificant, even impotent: "Oh, it's nothing – it's only my imagination." In truth, imagination sets energies in motion. It is a great tool of your creative self. Through this power, we can plug into a circuitry within that knows already that all is well.

You are remembering what you are imagining.

As you choose the perspective that you are already through the threshold, you stand in heaven on earth. You are that Being. You are limitlessly powerful and able to transform every experience you see. You are already bringing the loving solution into every dynamic, into every situation from the personal to the global. It's why you're here. You are the One.

When you see yourself this way, you begin to experience how it feels in the body. When we experience this in the body, we open to it and take action from this place. When we see and feel and sense and reveal ourselves as already through the threshold, we get to relax and celebrate in the truth of who we are. It is then that we truly serve.

Then we build circuitry in our system that maintains and sustains. And we build a reference, a model for others to see and resonate with. As we do this, the world shifts; it refines itself.

And as this occurs, we experience heaven on earth.

"As you choose the perspective that you are already through the threshold, you stand in heaven on earth."